A Christian High School Delight Directed Curriculum

90 guided lessons

Book 2

By: Laura Warden

Name:_____

Date:_____

Grade:_____

Instructions

This is a delighted directed book for your creative high school student. Have your student choose some books and write them down. Complete 6 pages a day to complete 90 days of guided lessons. This book is a little more structured for a more well rounded education, covering core subjects and electives.

High School Subjects
Bible

_____

Language Arts/Reading

_____

_____

History

_____

Science

_____

Math

_____

Internet Links

_____

_____

_____

2 Electives

_____

_____

Supplies
Pencils, erasers, gel pens, colored pencils, crayons, markers

Date :_____   Day 1

Bible Time

(Read for 20 min. in your bible)

Summarize in your own words what you read today.

_____

_____

_____

_____

_____

_____

_____

_____

_____

_____

_____

Scripture reference here.

_____

Language Arts/Literature
(Read or Study for 30 min.)

Topic of Study:_____

Notes, creative writing, summary, poetry

_____

_____

_____

_____

_____

_____

_____

_____

_____

_____

Vocabulary Look Up

_____

_____

_____

_____

_____

History

(Read for 20-30 min.)

Topic of Study:_____

What did you learn today?

_____

_____

_____

_____

_____

Draw a picture from your studies.

Science

(Read 20-30 min)

Topic of Study: _____

What did you learn today?

_____

_____

_____

_____

_____

_____

_____

Draw a picture from your studies.

Math

(Work for 45min-1hr)

Check when done_____

Use this page to work out problems.

Elective
(Work for 30 min)

Topic of Study:_____

Show an adult what you learned today. Write or draw about it here.

Elective
(Work for 30 min)

Topic of Study:_____

Show an adult what you learned today. Write or draw about it here.

Date :_____   Day 2

Bible Time

(Read for 20 min. in your bible)

Summarize in your own words what you read today.

_____

_____

_____

_____

_____

_____

_____

_____

_____

_____

_____

Scripture reference here.

_____

Language Arts/Literature

(Read or Study for 30 min.)

Topic of Study:_____

Notes, creative writing, summary, poetry

_____

_____

_____

_____

_____

_____

_____

_____

_____

_____

Vocabulary Look Up

_____

_____

_____

_____

_____

History

(Read for 20-30 min.)

Topic of Study:_____

What did you learn today?

_____

_____

_____

_____

_____

Draw a picture from your studies.

Science

(Read 20-30 min)

Topic of Study:_____

What did you learn today?

_____

_____

_____

_____

_____

_____

_____

Draw a picture from your studies.

Math

(Work for 45min-1hr)

Check when done_____

Use this page to work out problems.

Elective

(Work for 30 min)

Topic of Study:_____

Show an adult what you learned today. Write or draw about it here.

Elective

(Work for 30 min)

Topic of Study:_____

Show an adult what you learned today. Write or draw about it here.

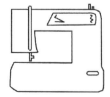

Date :_____   Day 3

Bible Time

(Read for 20 min. in your bible)

Summarize in your own words what you read today.

_____

_____

_____

_____

_____

_____

_____

_____

_____

_____

_____

_____

Scripture reference here.

_____

Language Arts/Literature

(Read or Study for 30 min.)

Topic of Study:_____

Notes, creative writing, summary, poetry

_____

_____

_____

_____

_____

_____

_____

_____

_____

Vocabulary Look Up

_____

_____

_____

_____

_____

History

(Read for 20-30 min.)

Topic of Study:_____

What did you learn today?

_____

_____

_____

_____

_____

Draw a picture from your studies.

Science

(Read 20-30 min)

Topic of Study:_____

What did you learn today?

_____

_____

_____

_____

_____

_____

_____

Draw a picture from your studies.

Math

(Work for 45min-1hr)

Check when done_____

Use this page to work out problems.

Elective

(Work for 30 min)

Topic of Study:_____

Show an adult what you learned today. Write or draw about it here.

Elective

(Work for 30 min)

Topic of Study:_____

Show an adult what you learned today. Write or draw about it here.

Date : _____   Day 4

Bible Time

(Read for 20 min. in your bible)

Summarize in your own words what you read today.

_____

_____

_____

_____

_____

_____

_____

_____

_____

_____

_____

_____

Scripture reference here.

_____

Language Arts/Literature

(Read or Study for 30 min.)

Topic of Study:_____

Notes, creative writing, summary, poetry

_____

_____

_____

_____

_____

_____

_____

_____

_____

_____

Vocabulary Look Up

_____

_____

_____

_____

_____

History

(Read for 20-30 min.)

Topic of Study:_____

What did you learn today?

_____

_____

_____

_____

_____

_____

Draw a picture from your studies.

Science

(Read 20-30 min)

Topic of Study:_____

What did you learn today?

_____

_____

_____

_____

_____

_____

_____

Draw a picture from your studies.

Math

(Work for 45min-1hr)

Check when done_____

Use this page to work out problems.

Elective
(Work for 30 min)

Topic of Study:_____

Show an adult what you learned today. Write or draw about it here.

Elective
(Work for 30 min)

Topic of Study:_____

Show an adult what you learned today. Write or draw about it here.

Date : _____   Day 5

Bible Time

(Read for 20 min. in your bible)

Summarize in your own words what you read today.

_____

_____

_____

_____

_____

_____

_____

_____

_____

_____

_____

_____

Scripture reference here.

_____

Language Arts/Literature
(Read or Study for 30 min.)

Topic of Study:_____

Notes, creative writing, summary, poetry

_____

_____

_____

_____

_____

_____

_____

_____

_____

_____

Vocabulary Look Up

_____

_____

_____

_____

_____

History

(Read for 20-30 min.)

Topic of Study:_____

What did you learn today?

_____

_____

_____

_____

_____

Draw a picture from your studies.

Science

(Read 20-30 min)

Topic of Study:_____

What did you learn today?

_____

_____

_____

_____

_____

_____

_____

Draw a picture from your studies.

Math

(Work for 45min-1hr)

Check when done_____

Use this page to work out problems.

Elective

(Work for 30 min)

Topic of Study:_____

Show an adult what you learned today. Write or draw about it here.

Elective

(Work for 30 min)

Topic of Study:_____

Show an adult what you learned today. Write or draw about it here.

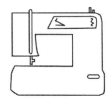

Date : _____   Day 6

Bible Time

(Read for 20 min. in your bible)

Summarize in your own words what you read today.

_____

_____

_____

_____

_____

_____

_____

_____

_____

_____

_____

Scripture reference here.

_____

Language Arts/Literature
(Read or Study for 30 min.)

Topic of Study:_____

Notes, creative writing, summary, poetry

_____

_____

_____

_____

_____

_____

_____

_____

_____

Vocabulary Look Up

_____

_____

_____

_____

_____

History

(Read for 20-30 min.)

Topic of Study:_____

What did you learn today?

_____

_____

_____

_____

_____

Draw a picture from your studies.

Science

(Read 20-30 min)

Topic of Study:_____

What did you learn today?

_____

_____

_____

_____

_____

_____

_____

Draw a picture from your studies.

Math

(Work for 45min-1hr)

Check when done_____

Use this page to work out problems.

Elective
(Work for 30 min)

Topic of Study:_____

Show an adult what you learned today. Write or draw about it here.

Elective
(Work for 30 min)

Topic of Study:_____

Show an adult what you learned today. Write or draw about it here.

Date : _____   Day 7

Bible Time

(Read for 20 min. in your bible)

Summarize in your own words what you read today.

_____

_____

_____

_____

_____

_____

_____

_____

_____

_____

_____

Scripture reference here.

_____

Language Arts/Literature

(Read or Study for 30 min.)

Topic of Study:_____

Notes, creative writing, summary, poetry

_____

_____

_____

_____

_____

_____

_____

_____

_____

Vocabulary Look Up

_____

_____

_____

_____

_____

History

(Read for 20-30 min.)

Topic of Study:_____

What did you learn today?

_____

_____

_____

_____

_____

Draw a picture from your studies.

Science

(Read 20-30 min)

Topic of Study:_____

What did you learn today?

_____

_____

_____

_____

_____

_____

_____

Draw a picture from your studies.

Math

(Work for 45min-1hr)

Check when done_____

Use this page to work out problems.

Elective

(Work for 30 min)

Topic of Study:_____

Show an adult what you learned today. Write or draw about it here.

Elective

(Work for 30 min)

Topic of Study:_____

Show an adult what you learned today. Write or draw about it here.

Date : _____   Day 8

Bible Time

(Read for 20 min. in your bible)

Summarize in your own words what you read today.

_____

_____

_____

_____

_____

_____

_____

_____

_____

_____

_____

_____

Scripture reference here.

_____

Language Arts/Literature

(Read or Study for 30 min.)

Topic of Study:_____

Notes, creative writing, summary, poetry

_____

_____

_____

_____

_____

_____

_____

_____

_____

Vocabulary Look Up

_____

_____

_____

_____

_____

History

(Read for 20-30 min.)

Topic of Study:_____

What did you learn today?

_____

_____

_____

_____

_____

_____

Draw a picture from your studies.

Science

(Read 20-30 min)

Topic of Study:_____

What did you learn today?

_____

_____

_____

_____

_____

_____

_____

Draw a picture from your studies.

Math

(Work for 45min-1hr)

Check when done_____

Use this page to work out problems.

Elective

(Work for 30 min)

Topic of Study:_____

Show an adult what you learned today. Write or draw about it here.

Elective

(Work for 30 min)

Topic of Study:_____

Show an adult what you learned today. Write or draw about it here.

Date :_____   Day 9

Bible Time

(Read for 20 min. in your bible)

Summarize in your own words what you read today.

_____

_____

_____

_____

_____

_____

_____

_____

_____

_____

_____

_____

Scripture reference here.

_____

Language Arts/Literature

(Read or Study for 30 min.)

Topic of Study:_____

Notes, creative writing, summary, poetry

_____

_____

_____

_____

_____

_____

_____

_____

_____

_____

Vocabulary Look Up

_____

_____

_____

_____

_____

History

(Read for 20-30 min.)

Topic of Study:_____

What did you learn today?

_____

_____

_____

_____

_____

_____

Draw a picture from your studies.

Science

(Read 20-30 min)

Topic of Study:_____

What did you learn today?

_____

_____

_____

_____

_____

_____

_____

Draw a picture from your studies.

Math

(Work for 45min-1hr)

Check when done_____

Use this page to work out problems.

Elective

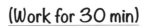

(Work for 30 min)

Topic of Study:_____

Show an adult what you learned today. Write or draw about it here.

Elective

(Work for 30 min)

Topic of Study:_____

Show an adult what you learned today. Write or draw about it here.

Date : _____   Day 10

Bible Time

(Read for 20 min. in your bible)

Summarize in your own words what you read today.

_____

_____

_____

_____

_____

_____

_____

_____

_____

_____

_____

Scripture reference here.

_____

Language Arts/Literature

(Read or Study for 30 min.)

Topic of Study:_____

Notes, creative writing, summary, poetry

_____

_____

_____

_____

_____

_____

_____

_____

_____

Vocabulary Look Up

_____

_____

_____

_____

History

(Read for 20-30 min.)

Topic of Study:_____

What did you learn today?

_____

_____

_____

_____

_____

_____

Draw a picture from your studies.

Science

(Read 20-30 min)

Topic of Study: _____

What did you learn today?

_____

_____

_____

_____

_____

_____

_____

Draw a picture from your studies.

Math

(Work for 45min-1hr)

Check when done_____

Use this page to work out problems.

Elective

(Work for 30 min)

Topic of Study:_____

Show an adult what you learned today. Write or draw about it here.

Elective

(Work for 30 min)

Topic of Study:_____

Show an adult what you learned today. Write or draw about it here.

Date :_____   Day 11

Bible Time

(Read for 20 min. in your bible)

Summarize in your own words what you read today.

_____

_____

_____

_____

_____

_____

_____

_____

_____

_____

_____

Scripture reference here.

_____

Language Arts/Literature

(Read or Study for 30 min.)

Topic of Study:_____

Notes, creative writing, summary, poetry

_____

_____

_____

_____

_____

_____

_____

_____

_____

Vocabulary Look Up

_____

_____

_____

_____

History

(Read for 20-30 min.)

Topic of Study:_____

What did you learn today?

_____

_____

_____

_____

_____

_____

Draw a picture from your studies.

Science

(Read 20-30 min)

Topic of Study:_____

What did you learn today?

_____

_____

_____

_____

_____

_____

_____

Draw a picture from your studies.

Math

(Work for 45min-1hr)

Check when done_____

Use this page to work out problems.

Elective

(Work for 30 min)

Topic of Study:_____

Show an adult what you learned today. Write or draw about it here.

Elective

(Work for 30 min)

Topic of Study:_____

Show an adult what you learned today. Write or draw about it here.

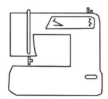

Date : _____   Day 12

Bible Time

(Read for 20 min. in your bible)

Summarize in your own words what you read today.

_____

_____

_____

_____

_____

_____

_____

_____

_____

_____

_____

_____

Scripture reference here.

_____

Language Arts/Literature
(Read or Study for 30 min.)

Topic of Study:_____

Notes, creative writing, summary, poetry

_____

_____

_____

_____

_____

_____

_____

_____

_____

_____

Vocabulary Look Up

_____

_____

_____

_____

_____

History

(Read for 20-30 min.)

Topic of Study:_____

What did you learn today?

_____

_____

_____

_____

_____

Draw a picture from your studies.

Science

(Read 20-30 min)

Topic of Study:_____

What did you learn today?

_____

_____

_____

_____

_____

_____

_____

Draw a picture from your studies.

Math

(Work for 45min-1hr)

Check when done_____

Use this page to work out problems.

Elective
(Work for 30 min)

Topic of Study:_____

Show an adult what you learned today. Write or draw about it here.

Elective
(Work for 30 min)

Topic of Study:_____

Show an adult what you learned today. Write or draw about it here.

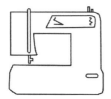

Date :_____   Day 13

Bible Time

(Read for 20 min. in your bible)

Summarize in your own words what you read today.

_____

_____

_____

_____

_____

_____

_____

_____

_____

_____

_____

Scripture reference here.

_____

Language Arts/Literature

(Read or Study for 30 min.)

Topic of Study:_____

Notes, creative writing, summary, poetry

_____

_____

_____

_____

_____

_____

_____

_____

_____

Vocabulary Look Up

_____

_____

_____

_____

_____

History

(Read for 20-30 min.)

Topic of Study:_____

What did you learn today?

_____

_____

_____

_____

_____

_____

Draw a picture from your studies.

Science

(Read 20-30 min)

Topic of Study:_____

What did you learn today?

_____

_____

_____

_____

_____

_____

_____

Draw a picture from your studies.

Math

(Work for 45min-1hr)

Check when done_____

Use this page to work out problems.

Elective
(Work for 30 min)

Topic of Study:_____

Show an adult what you learned today. Write or draw about it here.

Elective
(Work for 30 min)

Topic of Study:_____

Show an adult what you learned today. Write or draw about it here.

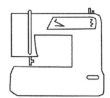

Date : _____   Day 14

Bible Time

(Read for 20 min. in your bible)

Summarize in your own words what you read today.

_____

_____

_____

_____

_____

_____

_____

_____

_____

_____

_____

Scripture reference here.

_____

Language Arts/Literature

(Read or Study for 30 min.)

Topic of Study:_____

Notes, creative writing, summary, poetry

_____

_____

_____

_____

_____

_____

_____

_____

_____

_____

Vocabulary Look Up

_____

_____

_____

_____

_____

History

(Read for 20-30 min.)

Topic of Study:_____

What did you learn today?

_____

_____

_____

_____

_____

_____

Draw a picture from your studies.

Science

(Read 20-30 min)

Topic of Study:_____

What did you learn today?

_____

_____

_____

_____

_____

_____

_____

Draw a picture from your studies.

Math

(Work for 45min-1hr)

Check when done_____

Use this page to work out problems.

Elective
(Work for 30 min)

Topic of Study:_____

Show an adult what you learned today. Write or draw about it here.

Elective
(Work for 30 min)

Topic of Study:_____

Show an adult what you learned today. Write or draw about it here.

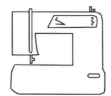

Date :_____   Day 15

Bible Time

(Read for 20 min. in your bible)

Summarize in your own words what you read today.

_____

_____

_____

_____

_____

_____

_____

_____

_____

_____

_____

Scripture reference here.

_____

Language Arts/Literature
(Read or Study for 30 min.)

Topic of Study:_____

Notes, creative writing, summary, poetry

_____

_____

_____

_____

_____

_____

_____

_____

_____

Vocabulary Look Up

_____

_____

_____

_____

History

(Read for 20-30 min.)

Topic of Study:_____

What did you learn today?

_____

_____

_____

_____

_____

_____

Draw a picture from your studies.

Science

(Read 20-30 min)

Topic of Study: _____

What did you learn today?

_____

_____

_____

_____

_____

_____

_____

Draw a picture from your studies.

Math

(Work for 45min-1hr)

Check when done_____

Use this page to work out problems.

Elective

(Work for 30 min)

Topic of Study:_____

Show an adult what you learned today. Write or draw about it here.

Elective

(Work for 30 min)

Topic of Study:_____

Show an adult what you learned today. Write or draw about it here.

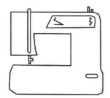

Date : _____   Day 16

Bible Time

(Read for 20 min. in your bible)

Summarize in your own words what you read today.

_____

_____

_____

_____

_____

_____

_____

_____

_____

_____

_____

_____

Scripture reference here.

_____

Language Arts/Literature
(Read or Study for 30 min.)

Topic of Study:_____

Notes, creative writing, summary, poetry

_____

_____

_____

_____

_____

_____

_____

_____

_____

_____

Vocabulary Look Up

_____

_____

_____

_____

_____

History

(Read for 20-30 min.)

Topic of Study: _____

What did you learn today?

_____

_____

_____

_____

_____

Draw a picture from your studies.

Science

(Read 20-30 min)

Topic of Study:_____

What did you learn today?

_____

_____

_____

_____

_____

_____

_____

Draw a picture from your studies.

Math

(Work for 45min-1hr)

Check when done_____

Use this page to work out problems.

Elective

(Work for 30 min)

Topic of Study:_____

Show an adult what you learned today. Write or draw about it here.

Elective

(Work for 30 min)

Topic of Study:_____

Show an adult what you learned today. Write or draw about it here.

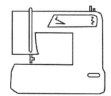

Date :_____   Day 17

Bible Time

(Read for 20 min. in your bible)

Summarize in your own words what you read today.

_____

_____

_____

_____

_____

_____

_____

_____

_____

_____

_____

_____

Scripture reference here.

_____

Language Arts/Literature
(Read or Study for 30 min.)

Topic of Study:_____

Notes, creative writing, summary, poetry

_____

_____

_____

_____

_____

_____

_____

_____

_____

Vocabulary Look Up

_____

_____

_____

_____

_____

History

(Read for 20-30 min.)

Topic of Study:_____

What did you learn today?

_____

_____

_____

_____

_____

Draw a picture from your studies.

Science

(Read 20-30 min)

Topic of Study:_____

What did you learn today?

_____

_____

_____

_____

_____

_____

_____

Draw a picture from your studies.

Math

(Work for 45min-1hr)

Check when done_____

Use this page to work out problems.

Elective

(Work for 30 min)

Topic of Study:_____

Show an adult what you learned today. Write or draw about it here.

Elective

(Work for 30 min)

Topic of Study:_____

Show an adult what you learned today. Write or draw about it here.

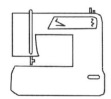

Date :_____   Day 18

Bible Time

(Read for 20 min. in your bible)

Summarize in your own words what you read today.

_____

_____

_____

_____

_____

_____

_____

_____

_____

_____

_____

Scripture reference here.

_____

Language Arts/Literature

(Read or Study for 30 min.)

Topic of Study:_____

Notes, creative writing, summary, poetry

_____

_____

_____

_____

_____

_____

_____

_____

_____

Vocabulary Look Up

_____

_____

_____

_____

_____

History

(Read for 20-30 min.)

Topic of Study:_____

What did you learn today?

_____

_____

_____

_____

_____

Draw a picture from your studies.

Science

(Read 20-30 min)

Topic of Study:_____

What did you learn today?

_____

_____

_____

_____

_____

_____

_____

_____

Draw a picture from your studies.

Math

(Work for 45min-1hr)

Check when done_____

Use this page to work out problems.

Elective

(Work for 30 min)

Topic of Study:_____

Show an adult what you learned today. Write or draw about it here.

Elective

(Work for 30 min)

Topic of Study:_____

Show an adult what you learned today. Write or draw about it here.

Date :_____   Day 19

Bible Time

(Read for 20 min. in your bible)

Summarize in your own words what you read today.

_____

_____

_____

_____

_____

_____

_____

_____

_____

_____

_____

Scripture reference here.

_____

Language Arts/Literature
(Read or Study for 30 min.)

Topic of Study:_____

Notes, creative writing, summary, poetry

_____

_____

_____

_____

_____

_____

_____

_____

_____

Vocabulary Look Up

_____

_____

_____

_____

History

(Read for 20-30 min.)

Topic of Study: _____

What did you learn today?

_____

_____

_____

_____

_____

Draw a picture from your studies.

Science

(Read 20-30 min)

Topic of Study: _____

What did you learn today?

_____

_____

_____

_____

_____

_____

_____

Draw a picture from your studies.

Math

(Work for 45min-1hr)

Check when done_____

Use this page to work out problems.

Elective

(Work for 30 min)

Topic of Study:_____

Show an adult what you learned today. Write or draw about it here.

Elective

(Work for 30 min)

Topic of Study:_____

Show an adult what you learned today. Write or draw about it here.

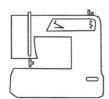

Date :_____   Day 20

Bible Time

(Read for 20 min. in your bible)

Summarize in your own words what you read today.

_____

_____

_____

_____

_____

_____

_____

_____

_____

_____

Scripture reference here.

_____

Language Arts/Literature
(Read or Study for 30 min.)

Topic of Study:_____

Notes, creative writing, summary, poetry

_____

_____

_____

_____

_____

_____

_____

_____

_____

Vocabulary Look Up

_____

_____

_____

_____

History

(Read for 20-30 min.)

Topic of Study:_____

What did you learn today?

_____

_____

_____

_____

_____

Draw a picture from your studies.

Science

(Read 20-30 min)

Topic of Study: _____

What did you learn today?

_____

_____

_____

_____

_____

_____

_____

Draw a picture from your studies.

Math

(Work for 45min-1hr)

Check when done_____

Use this page to work out problems.

Elective
(Work for 30 min)

Topic of Study:_____

Show an adult what you learned today. Write or draw about it here.

Elective
(Work for 30 min)

Topic of Study:_____

Show an adult what you learned today. Write or draw about it here.

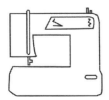

Date :_____   Day 21

Bible Time

(Read for 20 min. in your bible)

Summarize in your own words what you read today.

_____

_____

_____

_____

_____

_____

_____

_____

_____

_____

_____

Scripture reference here.

_____

Language Arts/Literature
(Read or Study for 30 min.)

Topic of Study:_____

Notes, creative writing, summary, poetry

_____

_____

_____

_____

_____

_____

_____

_____

_____

Vocabulary Look Up

_____

_____

_____

_____

History

(Read for 20-30 min.)

Topic of Study: _____

What did you learn today?

_____

_____

_____

_____

_____

Draw a picture from your studies.

Science

(Read 20-30 min)

Topic of Study:_____

What did you learn today?

_____

_____

_____

_____

_____

_____

_____

Draw a picture from your studies.

Math

(Work for 45min-1hr)

Check when done_____

Use this page to work out problems.

Elective

(Work for 30 min)

Topic of Study:_____

Show an adult what you learned today. Write or draw about it here.

Elective

(Work for 30 min)

Topic of Study:_____

Show an adult what you learned today. Write or draw about it here.

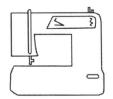

Date : _____   Day 22

Bible Time

(Read for 20 min. in your bible)

Summarize in your own words what you read today.

_____

_____

_____

_____

_____

_____

_____

_____

_____

_____

_____

Scripture reference here.

_____

Language Arts/Literature
(Read or Study for 30 min.)

Topic of Study:_____

Notes, creative writing, summary, poetry

_____

_____

_____

_____

_____

_____

_____

_____

_____

Vocabulary Look Up

_____

_____

_____

_____

_____

History

(Read for 20-30 min.)

Topic of Study:_____

What did you learn today?

_____

_____

_____

_____

_____

Draw a picture from your studies.

Science

(Read 20-30 min)

Topic of Study:_____

What did you learn today?

_____

_____

_____

_____

_____

_____

_____

Draw a picture from your studies.

Math

(Work for 45min-1hr)

Check when done_____

Use this page to work out problems.

Elective

(Work for 30 min)

Topic of Study:_____

Show an adult what you learned today. Write or draw about it here.

Elective

(Work for 30 min)

Topic of Study:_____

Show an adult what you learned today. Write or draw about it here.

Date :_____   Day 23

Bible Time

(Read for 20 min. in your bible)

Summarize in your own words what you read today.

_____

_____

_____

_____

_____

_____

_____

_____

_____

_____

_____

Scripture reference here.

_____

Language Arts/Literature

(Read or Study for 30 min.)

Topic of Study:_____

Notes, creative writing, summary, poetry

_____

_____

_____

_____

_____

_____

_____

_____

_____

Vocabulary Look Up

_____

_____

_____

_____

History

(Read for 20-30 min.)

Topic of Study:_____

What did you learn today?

_____

_____

_____

_____

_____

Draw a picture from your studies.

Science

(Read 20-30 min)

Topic of Study:_____

What did you learn today?

_____

_____

_____

_____

_____

_____

_____

Draw a picture from your studies.

Math

(Work for 45min-1hr)

Check when done_____

Use this page to work out problems.

Elective

(Work for 30 min)

Topic of Study:_____

Show an adult what you learned today. Write or draw about it here.

Elective

(Work for 30 min)

Topic of Study:_____

Show an adult what you learned today. Write or draw about it here.

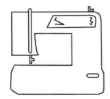

Date : _____   Day 24

Bible Time

(Read for 20 min. in your bible)

Summarize in your own words what you read today.

_____

_____

_____

_____

_____

_____

_____

_____

_____

_____

_____

Scripture reference here.

_____

Language Arts/Literature

(Read or Study for 30 min.)

Topic of Study:_____

Notes, creative writing, summary, poetry

_____

_____

_____

_____

_____

_____

_____

_____

_____

Vocabulary Look Up

_____

_____

_____

_____

_____

History

(Read for 20-30 min.)

Topic of Study:_____

What did you learn today?

_____

_____

_____

_____

_____

Draw a picture from your studies.

Science

(Read 20-30 min)

Topic of Study: _____

What did you learn today?

_____

_____

_____

_____

_____

_____

_____

Draw a picture from your studies.

Math

(Work for 45min-1hr)

Check when done_____

Use this page to work out problems.

Elective
(Work for 30 min)

Topic of Study:_____

Show an adult what you learned today. Write or draw about it here.

Elective
(Work for 30 min)

Topic of Study:_____

Show an adult what you learned today. Write or draw about it here.

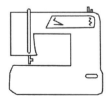

Date :_____   Day 25

Bible Time

(Read for 20 min. in your bible)

Summarize in your own words what you read today.

_____

_____

_____

_____

_____

_____

_____

_____

_____

_____

_____

Scripture reference here.

_____

Language Arts/Literature
(Read or Study for 30 min.)

Topic of Study:_____

Notes, creative writing, summary, poetry

_____
_____
_____
_____
_____
_____
_____
_____
_____

Vocabulary Look Up

_____
_____
_____
_____
_____

History

(Read for 20-30 min.)

Topic of Study:_____

What did you learn today?

_____

_____

_____

_____

_____

_____

Draw a picture from your studies.

Science

(Read 20-30 min)

Topic of Study:_____

What did you learn today?

_____

_____

_____

_____

_____

_____

_____

Draw a picture from your studies.

Math

(Work for 45min-1hr)

Check when done_____

Use this page to work out problems.

Elective

(Work for 30 min)

Topic of Study:_____

Show an adult what you learned today. Write or draw about it here.

Elective

(Work for 30 min)

Topic of Study:_____

Show an adult what you learned today. Write or draw about it here.

Date :_____   Day 26

Bible Time

(Read for 20 min. in your bible)

Summarize in your own words what you read today.

_____

_____

_____

_____

_____

_____

_____

_____

_____

_____

_____

_____

Scripture reference here.

_____

Language Arts/Literature

(Read or Study for 30 min.)

Topic of Study:_____

Notes, creative writing, summary, poetry

_____

_____

_____

_____

_____

_____

_____

_____

_____

_____

Vocabulary Look Up

_____

_____

_____

_____

_____

History

(Read for 20-30 min.)

Topic of Study:_____

What did you learn today?

_____

_____

_____

_____

_____

_____

Draw a picture from your studies.

Science

(Read 20-30 min)

Topic of Study: _____

What did you learn today?

_____

_____

_____

_____

_____

_____

_____

Draw a picture from your studies.

Math

(Work for 45min-1hr)

Check when done_____

Use this page to work out problems.

Elective

(Work for 30 min)

Topic of Study:_____

Show an adult what you learned today. Write or draw about it here.

Elective

(Work for 30 min)

Topic of Study:_____

Show an adult what you learned today. Write or draw about it here.

Date :_____   Day 27

Bible Time

(Read for 20 min. in your bible)

Summarize in your own words what you read today.

_____

_____

_____

_____

_____

_____

_____

_____

_____

_____

_____

Scripture reference here.

_____

Language Arts/Literature

(Read or Study for 30 min.)

Topic of Study:_____

Notes, creative writing, summary, poetry

_____

_____

_____

_____

_____

_____

_____

_____

_____

_____

Vocabulary Look Up

_____

_____

_____

_____

_____

History

(Read for 20-30 min.)

Topic of Study:_____

What did you learn today?

_____

_____

_____

_____

_____

_____

Draw a picture from your studies.

Science

(Read 20-30 min)

Topic of Study:_____

What did you learn today?

_____

_____

_____

_____

_____

_____

_____

Draw a picture from your studies.

Math

(Work for 45min-1hr)

Check when done_____

Use this page to work out problems.

Elective

(Work for 30 min)

Topic of Study:_____

Show an adult what you learned today. Write or draw about it here.

Elective

(Work for 30 min)

Topic of Study:_____

Show an adult what you learned today. Write or draw about it here.

Date :_____   Day 28

Bible Time

(Read for 20 min. in your bible)

Summarize in your own words what you read today.

_____

_____

_____

_____

_____

_____

_____

_____

_____

_____

_____

Scripture reference here.

_____

Language Arts/Literature

(Read or Study for 30 min.)

Topic of Study:_____

Notes, creative writing, summary, poetry

_____

_____

_____

_____

_____

_____

_____

_____

Vocabulary Look Up

_____

_____

_____

_____

History

(Read for 20-30 min.)

Topic of Study:_____

What did you learn today?

_____

_____

_____

_____

_____

_____

Draw a picture from your studies.

Science

(Read 20-30 min)

Topic of Study:_____

What did you learn today?

_____

_____

_____

_____

_____

_____

_____

Draw a picture from your studies.

Math

(Work for 45min-1hr)

Check when done_____

Use this page to work out problems.

Elective
(Work for 30 min)

Topic of Study:_____

Show an adult what you learned today. Write or draw about it here.

Elective
(Work for 30 min)

Topic of Study:_____

Show an adult what you learned today. Write or draw about it here.

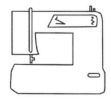

Date :_____ Day 29

Bible Time

(Read for 20 min. in your bible)

Summarize in your own words what you read today.

_____

_____

_____

_____

_____

_____

_____

_____

_____

_____

_____

_____

Scripture reference here.

_____

Language Arts/Literature

(Read or Study for 30 min.)

Topic of Study:_____

Notes, creative writing, summary, poetry

_____

_____

_____

_____

_____

_____

_____

_____

_____

_____

Vocabulary Look Up

_____

_____

_____

_____

_____

History

(Read for 20-30 min.)

Topic of Study:_____

What did you learn today?

_____

_____

_____

_____

_____

_____

Draw a picture from your studies.

Science

(Read 20-30 min)

Topic of Study:_____

What did you learn today?

_____

_____

_____

_____

_____

_____

_____

Draw a picture from your studies.

Math

(Work for 45min-1hr)

Check when done_____

Use this page to work out problems.

Elective
(Work for 30 min)

Topic of Study:_____

Show an adult what you learned today. Write or draw about it here.

Elective
(Work for 30 min)

Topic of Study:_____

Show an adult what you learned today. Write or draw about it here.

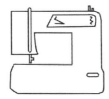

Bible Time

(Read for 20 min. in your bible)

Summarize in your own words what you read today.

_____

_____

_____

_____

_____

_____

_____

_____

_____

_____

_____

Scripture reference here.

_____

Language Arts/Literature

(Read or Study for 30 min.)

Topic of Study:_____

Notes, creative writing, summary, poetry

_____

_____

_____

_____

_____

_____

_____

_____

_____

Vocabulary Look Up

_____

_____

_____

_____

History

(Read for 20-30 min.)

Topic of Study:_____

What did you learn today?

_____

_____

_____

_____

_____

_____

Draw a picture from your studies.

Science

(Read 20-30 min)

Topic of Study:_____

What did you learn today?

_____

_____

_____

_____

_____

_____

_____

Draw a picture from your studies.

Math
(Work for 45min-1hr)
Check when done_____

Use this page to work out problems.

Elective

(Work for 30 min)

Topic of Study:_____

Show an adult what you learned today. Write or draw about it here.

Elective

(Work for 30 min)

Topic of Study:_____

Show an adult what you learned today. Write or draw about it here.

Date :_____   Day 31

Bible Time

(Read for 20 min. in your bible)

Summarize in your own words what you read today.

_____

_____

_____

_____

_____

_____

_____

_____

_____

_____

_____

Scripture reference here.

_____

Language Arts/Literature

(Read or Study for 30 min.)

Topic of Study:_____

Notes, creative writing, summary, poetry

_____

_____

_____

_____

_____

_____

_____

_____

_____

_____

Vocabulary Look Up

_____

_____

_____

_____

History

(Read for 20-30 min.)

Topic of Study:_____

What did you learn today?

_____

_____

_____

_____

_____

Draw a picture from your studies.

Science

(Read 20-30 min)

Topic of Study:_____

What did you learn today?

_____

_____

_____

_____

_____

_____

_____

Draw a picture from your studies.

Math

(Work for 45min-1hr)

Check when done_____

Use this page to work out problems.

Elective
(Work for 30 min)

Topic of Study:_____

Show an adult what you learned today. Write or draw about it here.

Elective
(Work for 30 min)

Topic of Study:_____

Show an adult what you learned today. Write or draw about it here.

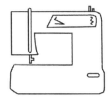

Date :_____   Day 32

Bible Time

(Read for 20 min. in your bible)

Summarize in your own words what you read today.

_____

_____

_____

_____

_____

_____

_____

_____

_____

_____

Scripture reference here.

_____

Language Arts/Literature

(Read or Study for 30 min.)

Topic of Study:_____

Notes, creative writing, summary, poetry

_____

_____

_____

_____

_____

_____

_____

_____

_____

_____

Vocabulary Look Up

_____

_____

_____

_____

History

(Read for 20-30 min.)

Topic of Study:_____

What did you learn today?

_____

_____

_____

_____

_____

Draw a picture from your studies.

Science

(Read 20-30 min)

Topic of Study:_____

What did you learn today?

_____

_____

_____

_____

_____

_____

_____

Draw a picture from your studies.

Math

(Work for 45min-1hr)

Check when done_____

Use this page to work out problems.

Elective
(Work for 30 min)

Topic of Study:_____

Show an adult what you learned today. Write or draw about it here.

Elective
(Work for 30 min)

Topic of Study:_____

Show an adult what you learned today. Write or draw about it here.

Date :_____   Day 33

Bible Time

(Read for 20 min. in your bible)

Summarize in your own words what you read today.

_____

_____

_____

_____

_____

_____

_____

_____

_____

_____

_____

Scripture reference here.

_____

Language Arts/Literature

(Read or Study for 30 min.)

Topic of Study:_____

Notes, creative writing, summary, poetry

_____

_____

_____

_____

_____

_____

_____

_____

_____

_____

Vocabulary Look Up

_____

_____

_____

_____

_____

History

(Read for 20-30 min.)

Topic of Study:_____

What did you learn today?

_____

_____

_____

_____

_____

Draw a picture from your studies.

Science

(Read 20-30 min)

Topic of Study:_____

What did you learn today?

_____

_____

_____

_____

_____

_____

_____

Draw a picture from your studies.

Math

(Work for 45min-1hr)

Check when done_____

Use this page to work out problems.

Elective

(Work for 30 min)

Topic of Study: _____

Show an adult what you learned today. Write or draw about it here.

Elective

(Work for 30 min)

Topic of Study: _____

Show an adult what you learned today. Write or draw about it here.

Date :_____   Day 34

Bible Time

(Read for 20 min. in your bible)

Summarize in your own words what you read today.

_____

_____

_____

_____

_____

_____

_____

_____

_____

_____

_____

Scripture reference here.

_____

Language Arts/Literature
(Read or Study for 30 min.)

Topic of Study:_____

Notes, creative writing, summary, poetry

_____

_____

_____

_____

_____

_____

_____

_____

_____

_____

Vocabulary Look Up

_____

_____

_____

_____

History

(Read for 20-30 min.)

Topic of Study:_____

What did you learn today?

_____

_____

_____

_____

_____

Draw a picture from your studies.

Science

(Read 20-30 min)

Topic of Study:_____

What did you learn today?

_____

_____

_____

_____

_____

_____

_____

Draw a picture from your studies.

Math

(Work for 45min-1hr)

Check when done_____

Use this page to work out problems.

Elective

(Work for 30 min)

Topic of Study:_____

Show an adult what you learned today. Write or draw about it here.

Elective

(Work for 30 min)

Topic of Study:_____

Show an adult what you learned today. Write or draw about it here.

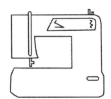

Date : _____   Day 35

Bible Time

(Read for 20 min. in your bible)

Summarize in your own words what you read today.

_____

_____

_____

_____

_____

_____

_____

_____

_____

_____

_____

Scripture reference here.

_____

Language Arts/Literature

(Read or Study for 30 min.)

Topic of Study:_____

Notes, creative writing, summary, poetry

_____

_____

_____

_____

_____

_____

_____

_____

_____

_____

Vocabulary Look Up

_____

_____

_____

_____

_____

History

(Read for 20-30 min.)

Topic of Study:_____

What did you learn today?

_____

_____

_____

_____

_____

_____

Draw a picture from your studies.

Science

(Read 20-30 min)

Topic of Study:_____

What did you learn today?

_____

_____

_____

_____

_____

_____

_____

Draw a picture from your studies.

Math

(Work for 45min-1hr)

Check when done_____

Use this page to work out problems.

Elective

(Work for 30 min)

Topic of Study:_____

Show an adult what you learned today. Write or draw about it here.

Elective

(Work for 30 min)

Topic of Study:_____

Show an adult what you learned today. Write or draw about it here.

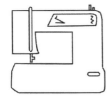

Bible Time

(Read for 20 min. in your bible)

Summarize in your own words what you read today.

_____

_____

_____

_____

_____

_____

_____

_____

_____

_____

_____

_____

Scripture reference here.

_____

Language Arts/Literature

(Read or Study for 30 min.)

Topic of Study:_____

Notes, creative writing, summary, poetry

_____

_____

_____

_____

_____

_____

_____

_____

_____

_____

Vocabulary Look Up

_____

_____

_____

_____

_____

History

(Read for 20-30 min.)

Topic of Study: _____

What did you learn today?

_____

_____

_____

_____

_____

Draw a picture from your studies.

Science

(Read 20-30 min)

Topic of Study:_____

What did you learn today?

_____

_____

_____

_____

_____

_____

_____

Draw a picture from your studies.

Math

(Work for 45min-1hr)

Check when done_____

Use this page to work out problems.

Elective

(Work for 30 min)

Topic of Study:_____

Show an adult what you learned today. Write or draw about it here.

Elective

(Work for 30 min)

Topic of Study:_____

Show an adult what you learned today. Write or draw about it here.

Date : _____   Day 37

Bible Time

(Read for 20 min. in your bible)

Summarize in your own words what you read today.

_____

_____

_____

_____

_____

_____

_____

_____

_____

_____

_____

Scripture reference here.

_____

Language Arts/Literature

(Read or Study for 30 min.)

Topic of Study:_____

Notes, creative writing, summary, poetry

_____

_____

_____

_____

_____

_____

_____

_____

_____

_____

Vocabulary Look Up

_____

_____

_____

_____

_____

History

(Read for 20-30 min.)

Topic of Study:_____

What did you learn today?

_____

_____

_____

_____

_____

Draw a picture from your studies.

Science

(Read 20-30 min)

Topic of Study:_____

What did you learn today?

_____

_____

_____

_____

_____

_____

_____

Draw a picture from your studies.

Math

(Work for 45min-1hr)

Check when done_____

Use this page to work out problems.

Elective

(Work for 30 min)

Topic of Study:_____

Show an adult what you learned today. Write or draw about it here.

Elective

(Work for 30 min)

Topic of Study:_____

Show an adult what you learned today. Write or draw about it here.

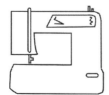

Date :_____   Day 38

Bible Time

(Read for 20 min. in your bible)

Summarize in your own words what you read today.

_____

_____

_____

_____

_____

_____

_____

_____

_____

_____

_____

_____

Scripture reference here.

_____

Language Arts/Literature

(Read or Study for 30 min.)

Topic of Study:_____

Notes, creative writing, summary, poetry

_____

_____

_____

_____

_____

_____

_____

_____

_____

Vocabulary Look Up

_____

_____

_____

_____

_____

History

(Read for 20-30 min.)

Topic of Study:_____

What did you learn today?

_____

_____

_____

_____

_____

Draw a picture from your studies.

Science

(Read 20-30 min)

Topic of Study:_____

What did you learn today?

_____

_____

_____

_____

_____

_____

_____

Draw a picture from your studies.

Math

(Work for 45min-1hr)

Check when done_____

Use this page to work out problems.

Elective
(Work for 30 min)

Topic of Study:_____

Show an adult what you learned today. Write or draw about it here.

Elective
(Work for 30 min)

Topic of Study:_____

Show an adult what you learned today. Write or draw about it here.

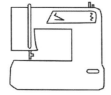

Date :_____   Day 39

Bible Time

(Read for 20 min. in your bible)

Summarize in your own words what you read today.

_____

_____

_____

_____

_____

_____

_____

_____

_____

_____

_____

_____

Scripture reference here.

_____

Language Arts/Literature

(Read or Study for 30 min.)

Topic of Study:_____

Notes, creative writing, summary, poetry

_____

_____

_____

_____

_____

_____

_____

_____

_____

Vocabulary Look Up

_____

_____

_____

_____

_____

History

(Read for 20-30 min.)

Topic of Study:_____

What did you learn today?

_____

_____

_____

_____

_____

Draw a picture from your studies.

Science

(Read 20-30 min)

Topic of Study:_____

What did you learn today?

_____

_____

_____

_____

_____

_____

_____

Draw a picture from your studies.

Math

(Work for 45min-1hr)

Check when done_____

Use this page to work out problems.

Elective

(Work for 30 min)

Topic of Study:_____

Show an adult what you learned today. Write or draw about it here.

Elective

(Work for 30 min)

Topic of Study:_____

Show an adult what you learned today. Write or draw about it here.

Date :_____   Day 40

Bible Time

(Read for 20 min. in your bible)

Summarize in your own words what you read today.

_____

_____

_____

_____

_____

_____

_____

_____

_____

_____

Scripture reference here.

_____

Language Arts/Literature

(Read or Study for 30 min.)

Topic of Study:_____

Notes, creative writing, summary, poetry

_____

_____

_____

_____

_____

_____

_____

_____

_____

_____

Vocabulary Look Up

_____

_____

_____

_____

History

(Read for 20-30 min.)

Topic of Study:_____

What did you learn today?

_____

_____

_____

_____

_____

Draw a picture from your studies.

Science

(Read 20-30 min)

Topic of Study:_____

What did you learn today?

_____

_____

_____

_____

_____

_____

_____

Draw a picture from your studies.

Math

(Work for 45min-1hr)

Check when done_____

Use this page to work out problems.

Elective

(Work for 30 min)

Topic of Study:_____

Show an adult what you learned today. Write or draw about it here.

Elective

(Work for 30 min)

Topic of Study:_____

Show an adult what you learned today. Write or draw about it here.

Date :_____   Day 41

Bible Time

(Read for 20 min. in your bible)

Summarize in your own words what you read today.

_____

_____

_____

_____

_____

_____

_____

_____

_____

_____

_____

_____

Scripture reference here.

_____

Language Arts/Literature

(Read or Study for 30 min.)

Topic of Study:_____

Notes, creative writing, summary, poetry

_____

_____

_____

_____

_____

_____

_____

_____

_____

_____

Vocabulary Look Up

_____

_____

_____

_____

_____

History

(Read for 20-30 min.)

Topic of Study:_____

What did you learn today?

_____

_____

_____

_____

_____

Draw a picture from your studies.

Science

(Read 20-30 min)

Topic of Study:_____

What did you learn today?

_____

_____

_____

_____

_____

_____

_____

Draw a picture from your studies.

Math

(Work for 45min-1hr)

Check when done_____

Use this page to work out problems.

Elective

(Work for 30 min)

Topic of Study:_____

Show an adult what you learned today. Write or draw about it here.

Elective

(Work for 30 min)

Topic of Study:_____

Show an adult what you learned today. Write or draw about it here.

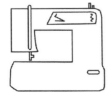

Date :_____   Day 42

Bible Time

(Read for 20 min. in your bible)

Summarize in your own words what you read today.

_____

_____

_____

_____

_____

_____

_____

_____

_____

_____

_____

_____

Scripture reference here.

_____

Language Arts/Literature

(Read or Study for 30 min.)

Topic of Study:_____

Notes, creative writing, summary, poetry

_____

_____

_____

_____

_____

_____

_____

_____

_____

_____

Vocabulary Look Up

_____

_____

_____

_____

History

(Read for 20-30 min.)

Topic of Study:_____

What did you learn today?

_____

_____

_____

_____

_____

Draw a picture from your studies.

Science

(Read 20-30 min)

Topic of Study: _____

What did you learn today?

_____

_____

_____

_____

_____

_____

_____

Draw a picture from your studies.

Math

(Work for 45min-1hr)

Check when done_____

Use this page to work out problems.

Elective

(Work for 30 min)

Topic of Study:_____

Show an adult what you learned today. Write or draw about it here.

Elective

(Work for 30 min)

Topic of Study:_____

Show an adult what you learned today. Write or draw about it here.

Date :_____   Day 43

Bible Time

(Read for 20 min. in your bible)

Summarize in your own words what you read today.

_____

_____

_____

_____

_____

_____

_____

_____

_____

_____

_____

_____

Scripture reference here.

_____

Language Arts/Literature

(Read or Study for 30 min.)

Topic of Study:_____

Notes, creative writing, summary, poetry

_____

_____

_____

_____

_____

_____

_____

_____

_____

Vocabulary Look Up

_____

_____

_____

_____

_____

History

(Read for 20-30 min.)

Topic of Study:_____

What did you learn today?

_____

_____

_____

_____

_____

Draw a picture from your studies.

Science

(Read 20-30 min)

Topic of Study:_____

What did you learn today?

_____

_____

_____

_____

_____

_____

_____

Draw a picture from your studies.

Math

(Work for 45min-1hr)

Check when done_____

Use this page to work out problems.

Elective

(Work for 30 min)

Topic of Study:_____

Show an adult what you learned today. Write or draw about it here.

Elective

(Work for 30 min)

Topic of Study:_____

Show an adult what you learned today. Write or draw about it here.

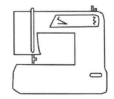

Date :_____   Day 44

Bible Time

(Read for 20 min. in your bible)

Summarize in your own words what you read today.

_____

_____

_____

_____

_____

_____

_____

_____

_____

_____

_____

_____

Scripture reference here.

_____

Language Arts/Literature

(Read or Study for 30 min.)

Topic of Study:_____

Notes, creative writing, summary, poetry

_____

_____

_____

_____

_____

_____

_____

_____

_____

Vocabulary Look Up

_____

_____

_____

_____

History

(Read for 20-30 min.)

Topic of Study:_____

What did you learn today?

_____

_____

_____

_____

_____

Draw a picture from your studies.

Science

(Read 20-30 min)

Topic of Study:_____

What did you learn today?

_____

_____

_____

_____

_____

_____

_____

Draw a picture from your studies.

Math

(Work for 45min-1hr)

Check when done_____

Use this page to work out problems.

Elective

(Work for 30 min)

Topic of Study:_____

Show an adult what you learned today. Write or draw about it here.

Elective

(Work for 30 min)

Topic of Study:_____

Show an adult what you learned today. Write or draw about it here.

Date : _____   Day 45

Bible Time

(Read for 20 min. in your bible)

Summarize in your own words what you read today.

_____

_____

_____

_____

_____

_____

_____

_____

_____

_____

_____

Scripture reference here.

_____

Language Arts/Literature
(Read or Study for 30 min.)

Topic of Study:_____

Notes, creative writing, summary, poetry

_____
_____
_____
_____
_____
_____
_____
_____
_____
_____
_____
_____

Vocabulary Look Up

_____
_____
_____
_____
_____

History

(Read for 20-30 min.)

Topic of Study:_____

What did you learn today?

_____

_____

_____

_____

_____

Draw a picture from your studies.

Science
(Read 20-30 min)

Topic of Study:_____

What did you learn today?

_____

_____

_____

_____

_____

_____

_____

Draw a picture from your studies.

Math

(Work for 45min-1hr)

Check when done_____

Use this page to work out problems.

Elective

(Work for 30 min)

Topic of Study:_____

Show an adult what you learned today. Write or draw about it here.

Elective

(Work for 30 min)

Topic of Study:_____

Show an adult what you learned today. Write or draw about it here.

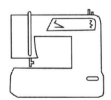

Date :_____   Day 46

Bible Time

(Read for 20 min. in your bible)

Summarize in your own words what you read today.

_____

_____

_____

_____

_____

_____

_____

_____

_____

_____

_____

Scripture reference here.

_____

Language Arts/Literature

(Read or Study for 30 min.)

Topic of Study:_____

Notes, creative writing, summary, poetry

_____

_____

_____

_____

_____

_____

_____

_____

Vocabulary Look Up

_____

_____

_____

_____

History

(Read for 20-30 min.)

Topic of Study:_____

What did you learn today?

_____

_____

_____

_____

_____

_____

Draw a picture from your studies.

Science
(Read 20-30 min)

Topic of Study:_____

What did you learn today?

_____

_____

_____

_____

_____

_____

_____

Draw a picture from your studies.

Math

(Work for 45min-1hr)

Check when done_____

Use this page to work out problems.

Elective

(Work for 30 min)

Topic of Study:_____

Show an adult what you learned today. Write or draw about it here.

Elective

(Work for 30 min)

Topic of Study:_____

Show an adult what you learned today. Write or draw about it here.

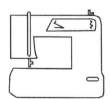

Date : _____   Day 47

Bible Time

(Read for 20 min. in your bible)

Summarize in your own words what you read today.

_____

_____

_____

_____

_____

_____

_____

_____

_____

_____

_____

_____

Scripture reference here.

_____

Language Arts/Literature

(Read or Study for 30 min.)

Topic of Study:_____

Notes, creative writing, summary, poetry

_____

_____

_____

_____

_____

_____

_____

_____

_____

_____

Vocabulary Look Up

_____

_____

_____

_____

_____

History
(Read for 20-30 min.)

Topic of Study:_____

What did you learn today?

_____

_____

_____

_____

_____

_____

Draw a picture from your studies.

Science

(Read 20-30 min)

Topic of Study:_____

What did you learn today?

_____

_____

_____

_____

_____

_____

_____

Draw a picture from your studies.

Math

(Work for 45min-1hr)

Check when done_____

Use this page to work out problems.

Elective

(Work for 30 min)

Topic of Study:_____

Show an adult what you learned today. Write or draw about it here.

Elective

(Work for 30 min)

Topic of Study:_____

Show an adult what you learned today. Write or draw about it here.

Date :_____   Day 48

Bible Time

(Read for 20 min. in your bible)

Summarize in your own words what you read today.

_____

_____

_____

_____

_____

_____

_____

_____

_____

_____

_____

_____

Scripture reference here.

_____

Language Arts/Literature

(Read or Study for 30 min.)

Topic of Study:_____

Notes, creative writing, summary, poetry

_____

_____

_____

_____

_____

_____

_____

_____

_____

_____

Vocabulary Look Up

_____

_____

_____

_____

_____

History

(Read for 20-30 min.)

Topic of Study:_____

What did you learn today?

_____

_____

_____

_____

_____

Draw a picture from your studies.

Science

(Read 20-30 min)

Topic of Study: _____

What did you learn today?

_____

_____

_____

_____

_____

_____

_____

Draw a picture from your studies.

Math

(Work for 45min-1hr)

Check when done_____

Use this page to work out problems.

Elective

(Work for 30 min)

Topic of Study:_____

Show an adult what you learned today. Write or draw about it here.

Elective

(Work for 30 min)

Topic of Study:_____

Show an adult what you learned today. Write or draw about it here.

Date :_____ Day 49

Bible Time

(Read for 20 min. in your bible)

Summarize in your own words what you read today.

_____

_____

_____

_____

_____

_____

_____

_____

_____

_____

_____

Scripture reference here.

_____

Language Arts/Literature

(Read or Study for 30 min.)

Topic of Study:_____

Notes, creative writing, summary, poetry

_____

_____

_____

_____

_____

_____

_____

_____

_____

_____

Vocabulary Look Up

_____

_____

_____

_____

_____

History

(Read for 20-30 min.)

Topic of Study:_____

What did you learn today?

_____

_____

_____

_____

_____

Draw a picture from your studies.

Science

(Read 20-30 min)

Topic of Study:_____

What did you learn today?

_____

_____

_____

_____

_____

_____

_____

Draw a picture from your studies.

Math

(Work for 45min-1hr)

Check when done_____

Use this page to work out problems.

Elective

(Work for 30 min)

Topic of Study:_____

Show an adult what you learned today. Write or draw about it here.

Elective

(Work for 30 min)

Topic of Study:_____

Show an adult what you learned today. Write or draw about it here.

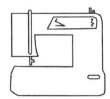

Date :_____   Day 50

Bible Time

(Read for 20 min. in your bible)

Summarize in your own words what you read today.

_____

_____

_____

_____

_____

_____

_____

_____

_____

_____

_____

Scripture reference here.

_____

Language Arts/Literature
(Read or Study for 30 min.)

Topic of Study:_____

Notes, creative writing, summary, poetry

_____

_____

_____

_____

_____

_____

_____

_____

_____

Vocabulary Look Up

_____

_____

_____

_____

_____

History

(Read for 20-30 min.)

Topic of Study:_____

What did you learn today?

_____

_____

_____

_____

_____

Draw a picture from your studies.

Science

(Read 20-30 min)

Topic of Study:_____

What did you learn today?

_____

_____

_____

_____

_____

_____

_____

Draw a picture from your studies.

Math

(Work for 45min-1hr)

Check when done_____

Use this page to work out problems.

Elective

(Work for 30 min)

Topic of Study:_____

Show an adult what you learned today. Write or draw about it here.

Elective

(Work for 30 min)

Topic of Study:_____

Show an adult what you learned today. Write or draw about it here.

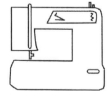

Date :_____   Day 51

Bible Time

(Read for 20 min. in your bible)

Summarize in your own words what you read today.

_____
_____
_____
_____
_____
_____
_____
_____
_____
_____
_____

Scripture reference here.

_____

Language Arts/Literature

(Read or Study for 30 min.)

Topic of Study:_____

Notes, creative writing, summary, poetry

_____

_____

_____

_____

_____

_____

_____

_____

_____

_____

Vocabulary Look Up

_____

_____

_____

_____

_____

History

(Read for 20-30 min.)

Topic of Study:_____

What did you learn today?

_____

_____

_____

_____

_____

Draw a picture from your studies.

Science

(Read 20-30 min)

Topic of Study:_____

What did you learn today?

_____

_____

_____

_____

_____

_____

_____

Draw a picture from your studies.

Math

(Work for 45min-1hr)

Check when done_____

Use this page to work out problems.

Elective

(Work for 30 min)

Topic of Study:_____

Show an adult what you learned today. Write or draw about it here.

Elective

(Work for 30 min)

Topic of Study:_____

Show an adult what you learned today. Write or draw about it here.

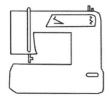

Date : _____   Day 52

Bible Time

(Read for 20 min. in your bible)

Summarize in your own words what you read today.

_____

_____

_____

_____

_____

_____

_____

_____

_____

_____

_____

Scripture reference here.

_____

Language Arts/Literature

(Read or Study for 30 min.)

Topic of Study:_____

Notes, creative writing, summary, poetry

_____

_____

_____

_____

_____

_____

_____

_____

_____

Vocabulary Look Up

_____

_____

_____

_____

_____

History

(Read for 20-30 min.)

Topic of Study:_____

What did you learn today?

_____

_____

_____

_____

_____

Draw a picture from your studies.

Science
(Read 20-30 min)

Topic of Study:_____

What did you learn today?

_____

_____

_____

_____

_____

_____

_____

Draw a picture from your studies.

Math

(Work for 45min-1hr)

Check when done_____

Use this page to work out problems.

Elective
(Work for 30 min)

Topic of Study: _____

Show an adult what you learned today. Write or draw about it here.

Elective
(Work for 30 min)

Topic of Study: _____

Show an adult what you learned today. Write or draw about it here.

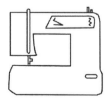

Date :_____   Day 53

Bible Time

(Read for 20 min. in your bible)

Summarize in your own words what you read today.

_____

_____

_____

_____

_____

_____

_____

_____

_____

_____

_____

_____

Scripture reference here.

_____

Language Arts/Literature

(Read or Study for 30 min.)

Topic of Study:_____

Notes, creative writing, summary, poetry

_____

_____

_____

_____

_____

_____

_____

_____

Vocabulary Look Up

_____

_____

_____

_____

_____

History
(Read for 20-30 min.)

Topic of Study:_____

What did you learn today?

_____

_____

_____

_____

_____

Draw a picture from your studies.

Science

(Read 20-30 min)

Topic of Study:_____

What did you learn today?

_____

_____

_____

_____

_____

_____

_____

Draw a picture from your studies.

Math

(Work for 45min-1hr)

Check when done_____

Use this page to work out problems.

Elective
(Work for 30 min)

Topic of Study:_____

Show an adult what you learned today. Write or draw about it here.

Elective
(Work for 30 min)

Topic of Study:_____

Show an adult what you learned today. Write or draw about it here.

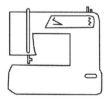

Date :_____   Day 54

Bible Time

(Read for 20 min. in your bible)

Summarize in your own words what you read today.

_____

_____

_____

_____

_____

_____

_____

_____

_____

_____

_____

Scripture reference here.

_____

Language Arts/Literature

(Read or Study for 30 min.)

Topic of Study:_____

Notes, creative writing, summary, poetry

_____

_____

_____

_____

_____

_____

_____

_____

_____

Vocabulary Look Up

_____

_____

_____

_____

_____

History
(Read for 20-30 min.)

Topic of Study:_____

What did you learn today?

_____

_____

_____

_____

_____

Draw a picture from your studies.

Science

(Read 20-30 min)

Topic of Study:_____

What did you learn today?

_____

_____

_____

_____

_____

_____

_____

Draw a picture from your studies.

Math

(Work for 45min-1hr)

Check when done_____

Use this page to work out problems.

Elective
(Work for 30 min)

Topic of Study:_____

Show an adult what you learned today. Write or draw about it here.

Elective
(Work for 30 min)

Topic of Study:_____

Show an adult what you learned today. Write or draw about it here.

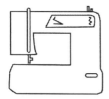

Date :_____   Day 55

Bible Time

(Read for 20 min. in your bible)

Summarize in your own words what you read today.

_____

_____

_____

_____

_____

_____

_____

_____

_____

_____

_____

_____

Scripture reference here.

_____

Language Arts/Literature

(Read or Study for 30 min.)

Topic of Study:_____

Notes, creative writing, summary, poetry

_____

_____

_____

_____

_____

_____

_____

_____

_____

Vocabulary Look Up

_____

_____

_____

_____

History

(Read for 20-30 min.)

Topic of Study:_____

What did you learn today?

_____

_____

_____

_____

_____

_____

Draw a picture from your studies.

Science

(Read 20-30 min)

Topic of Study:_____

What did you learn today?

_____
_____
_____
_____
_____
_____
_____

Draw a picture from your studies.

Math

(Work for 45min-1hr)

Check when done_____

Use this page to work out problems.

Elective
(Work for 30 min)

Topic of Study:_____

Show an adult what you learned today. Write or draw about it here.

Elective
(Work for 30 min)

Topic of Study:_____

Show an adult what you learned today. Write or draw about it here.

Date :_____   Day 56

Bible Time

(Read for 20 min. in your bible)

Summarize in your own words what you read today.

_____

_____

_____

_____

_____

_____

_____

_____

_____

_____

_____

_____

Scripture reference here.

_____

Language Arts/Literature

(Read or Study for 30 min.)

Topic of Study:_____

Notes, creative writing, summary, poetry

_____

_____

_____

_____

_____

_____

_____

_____

_____

Vocabulary Look Up

_____

_____

_____

_____

History

(Read for 20-30 min.)

Topic of Study:_____

What did you learn today?

_____

_____

_____

_____

_____

Draw a picture from your studies.

Science

(Read 20-30 min)

Topic of Study:_____

What did you learn today?

_____

_____

_____

_____

_____

_____

_____

Draw a picture from your studies.

Math

(Work for 45min-1hr)

Check when done_____

Use this page to work out problems.

Elective

(Work for 30 min)

Topic of Study:_____

Show an adult what you learned today. Write or draw about it here.

Elective

(Work for 30 min)

Topic of Study:_____

Show an adult what you learned today. Write or draw about it here.

Date :_____   Day 57

Bible Time

(Read for 20 min. in your bible)

Summarize in your own words what you read today.

_____

_____

_____

_____

_____

_____

_____

_____

_____

_____

_____

_____

Scripture reference here.

_____

Language Arts/Literature
(Read or Study for 30 min.)

Topic of Study:_____

Notes, creative writing, summary, poetry

_____

_____

_____

_____

_____

_____

_____

_____

_____

Vocabulary Look Up

_____

_____

_____

_____

History

(Read for 20-30 min.)

Topic of Study:_____

What did you learn today?

_____

_____

_____

_____

_____

Draw a picture from your studies.

Science

(Read 20-30 min)

Topic of Study:_____

What did you learn today?

_____

_____

_____

_____

_____

_____

_____

Draw a picture from your studies.

Math

(Work for 45min-1hr)

Check when done_____

Use this page to work out problems.

Elective

(Work for 30 min)

Topic of Study:_____

Show an adult what you learned today. Write or draw about it here.

Elective

(Work for 30 min)

Topic of Study:_____

Show an adult what you learned today. Write or draw about it here.

Date :_____   Day 58

Bible Time

(Read for 20 min. in your bible)

Summarize in your own words what you read today.

_____

_____

_____

_____

_____

_____

_____

_____

_____

_____

_____

Scripture reference here.

_____

Language Arts/Literature

(Read or Study for 30 min.)

Topic of Study:_____

Notes, creative writing, summary, poetry

_____

_____

_____

_____

_____

_____

_____

_____

_____

_____

Vocabulary Look Up

_____

_____

_____

_____

_____

History

(Read for 20-30 min.)

Topic of Study:_____

What did you learn today?

_____

_____

_____

_____

_____

Draw a picture from your studies.

Science

(Read 20-30 min)

Topic of Study:_____

What did you learn today?

_____

_____

_____

_____

_____

_____

_____

Draw a picture from your studies.

Math

(Work for 45min-1hr)

Check when done_____

Use this page to work out problems.

Elective

(Work for 30 min)

Topic of Study:_____

Show an adult what you learned today. Write or draw about it here.

Elective

(Work for 30 min)

Topic of Study:_____

Show an adult what you learned today. Write or draw about it here.

Date :_____   Day 59

Bible Time

(Read for 20 min. in your bible)

Summarize in your own words what you read today.

_____

_____

_____

_____

_____

_____

_____

_____

_____

_____

_____

Scripture reference here.

_____

Language Arts/Literature

(Read or Study for 30 min.)

Topic of Study:_____

Notes, creative writing, summary, poetry

_____

_____

_____

_____

_____

_____

_____

_____

_____

Vocabulary Look Up

_____

_____

_____

_____

_____

History

(Read for 20-30 min.)

Topic of Study:_____

What did you learn today?

_____

_____

_____

_____

_____

_____

Draw a picture from your studies.

Science

(Read 20-30 min)

Topic of Study: _____

What did you learn today?

_____

_____

_____

_____

_____

_____

_____

Draw a picture from your studies.

Math

(Work for 45min-1hr)

Check when done_____

Use this page to work out problems.

Elective

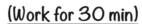

(Work for 30 min)

Topic of Study:_____

Show an adult what you learned today. Write or draw about it here.

Elective

(Work for 30 min)

Topic of Study:_____

Show an adult what you learned today. Write or draw about it here.

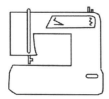

Date :_____   Day 60

Bible Time

(Read for 20 min. in your bible)

Summarize in your own words what you read today.

_____

_____

_____

_____

_____

_____

_____

_____

_____

_____

_____

_____

Scripture reference here.

_____

Language Arts/Literature
(Read or Study for 30 min.)

Topic of Study:_____

Notes, creative writing, summary, poetry

_____

_____

_____

_____

_____

_____

_____

_____

_____

Vocabulary Look Up

_____

_____

_____

_____

History

(Read for 20-30 min.)

Topic of Study:_____

What did you learn today?

_____

_____

_____

_____

_____

_____

Draw a picture from your studies.

Science

(Read 20-30 min)

Topic of Study:_____

What did you learn today?

_____

_____

_____

_____

_____

_____

_____

Draw a picture from your studies.

Math

(Work for 45min-1hr)

Check when done_____

Use this page to work out problems.

Elective

(Work for 30 min)

Topic of Study:_____

Show an adult what you learned today. Write or draw about it here.

Elective

(Work for 30 min)

Topic of Study:_____

Show an adult what you learned today. Write or draw about it here.

Date :_____   Day 61

Bible Time

(Read for 20 min. in your bible)

Summarize in your own words what you read today.

_____
_____
_____
_____
_____
_____
_____
_____
_____
_____
_____

Scripture reference here.

_____

Language Arts/Literature

(Read or Study for 30 min.)

Topic of Study:_____

Notes, creative writing, summary, poetry

_____

_____

_____

_____

_____

_____

_____

_____

_____

_____

Vocabulary Look Up

_____

_____

_____

_____

_____

History

(Read for 20-30 min.)

Topic of Study:_____

What did you learn today?

_____

_____

_____

_____

_____

_____

Draw a picture from your studies.

Science

(Read 20-30 min)

Topic of Study:_____

What did you learn today?

_____

_____

_____

_____

_____

_____

_____

Draw a picture from your studies.

Math

(Work for 45min-1hr)

Check when done_____

Use this page to work out problems.

Elective

(Work for 30 min)

Topic of Study:_____

Show an adult what you learned today. Write or draw about it here.

Elective

(Work for 30 min)

Topic of Study:_____

Show an adult what you learned today. Write or draw about it here.

Date : _____   Day 62

Bible Time

(Read for 20 min. in your bible)

Summarize in your own words what you read today.

_____

_____

_____

_____

_____

_____

_____

_____

_____

_____

_____

_____

Scripture reference here.

_____

Language Arts/Literature

(Read or Study for 30 min.)

Topic of Study:_____

Notes, creative writing, summary, poetry

_____

_____

_____

_____

_____

_____

_____

_____

_____

Vocabulary Look Up

_____

_____

_____

_____

_____

History

(Read for 20-30 min.)

Topic of Study:_____

What did you learn today?

_____

_____

_____

_____

_____

_____

Draw a picture from your studies.

Science

(Read 20-30 min)

Topic of Study:_____

What did you learn today?

_____

_____

_____

_____

_____

_____

_____

Draw a picture from your studies.

Math

(Work for 45min-1hr)

Check when done_____

Use this page to work out problems.

Elective

(Work for 30 min)

Topic of Study:_____

Show an adult what you learned today. Write or draw about it here.

Elective

(Work for 30 min)

Topic of Study:_____

Show an adult what you learned today. Write or draw about it here.

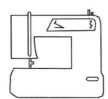

Date :_____   Day 63

Bible Time

(Read for 20 min. in your bible)

Summarize in your own words what you read today.

_____
_____
_____
_____
_____
_____
_____
_____
_____
_____
_____
_____

Scripture reference here.

_____

Language Arts/Literature

(Read or Study for 30 min.)

Topic of Study:_____

Notes, creative writing, summary, poetry

_____

_____

_____

_____

_____

_____

_____

_____

_____

Vocabulary Look Up

_____

_____

_____

_____

History

(Read for 20-30 min.)

Topic of Study:_____

What did you learn today?

_____

_____

_____

_____

_____

Draw a picture from your studies.

Science

(Read 20-30 min)

Topic of Study: _____

What did you learn today?

_____

_____

_____

_____

_____

_____

_____

Draw a picture from your studies.

Math

(Work for 45min-1hr)

Check when done_____

Use this page to work out problems.

Elective
(Work for 30 min)

Topic of Study:_____

Show an adult what you learned today. Write or draw about it here.

Elective
(Work for 30 min)

Topic of Study:_____

Show an adult what you learned today. Write or draw about it here.

Date :_____   Day 64

Bible Time

(Read for 20 min. in your bible)

Summarize in your own words what you read today.

_____
_____
_____
_____
_____
_____
_____
_____
_____
_____
_____
_____

Scripture reference here.

_____

Language Arts/Literature

(Read or Study for 30 min.)

Topic of Study:_____

Notes, creative writing, summary, poetry

_____

_____

_____

_____

_____

_____

_____

_____

_____

Vocabulary Look Up

_____

_____

_____

_____

History

(Read for 20-30 min.)

Topic of Study:_____

What did you learn today?

_____

_____

_____

_____

_____

Draw a picture from your studies.

Science

(Read 20-30 min)

Topic of Study:_____

What did you learn today?

_____

_____

_____

_____

_____

_____

_____

Draw a picture from your studies.

Math

(Work for 45min-1hr)

Check when done_____

Use this page to work out problems.

Elective
(Work for 30 min)

Topic of Study:_____

Show an adult what you learned today. Write or draw about it here.

Elective
(Work for 30 min)

Topic of Study:_____

Show an adult what you learned today. Write or draw about it here.

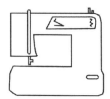

Date :_____   Day 65

Bible Time

(Read for 20 min. in your bible)

Summarize in your own words what you read today.

_____

_____

_____

_____

_____

_____

_____

_____

_____

_____

_____

Scripture reference here.

_____

Language Arts/Literature

(Read or Study for 30 min.)

Topic of Study:_____

Notes, creative writing, summary, poetry

_____

_____

_____

_____

_____

_____

_____

_____

_____

Vocabulary Look Up

_____

_____

_____

_____

_____

History

(Read for 20-30 min.)

Topic of Study:_____

What did you learn today?

_____

_____

_____

_____

_____

_____

Draw a picture from your studies.

Science

(Read 20-30 min)

Topic of Study:_____

What did you learn today?

_____

_____

_____

_____

_____

_____

_____

Draw a picture from your studies.

Math

(Work for 45min-1hr)

Check when done_____

Use this page to work out problems.

Elective

(Work for 30 min)

Topic of Study:_____

Show an adult what you learned today. Write or draw about it here.

Elective

(Work for 30 min)

Topic of Study:_____

Show an adult what you learned today. Write or draw about it here.

Date : _____   Day 66

Bible Time

(Read for 20 min. in your bible)

Summarize in your own words what you read today.

_____

_____

_____

_____

_____

_____

_____

_____

_____

_____

_____

Scripture reference here.

_____

Language Arts/Literature

(Read or Study for 30 min.)

Topic of Study:_____

Notes, creative writing, summary, poetry

_____

_____

_____

_____

_____

_____

_____

_____

_____

_____

Vocabulary Look Up

_____

_____

_____

_____

_____

History
(Read for 20-30 min.)

Topic of Study:_____

What did you learn today?

_____

_____

_____

_____

_____

Draw a picture from your studies.

Science

(Read 20-30 min)

Topic of Study:_____

What did you learn today?

_____

_____

_____

_____

_____

_____

_____

Draw a picture from your studies.

Math

(Work for 45min-1hr)

Check when done_____

Use this page to work out problems.

Elective
(Work for 30 min)

Topic of Study:_____

Show an adult what you learned today. Write or draw about it here.

Elective
(Work for 30 min)

Topic of Study:_____

Show an adult what you learned today. Write or draw about it here.

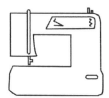

Date :_____   Day 67

Bible Time

(Read for 20 min. in your bible)

Summarize in your own words what you read today.

_____

_____

_____

_____

_____

_____

_____

_____

_____

_____

_____

_____

Scripture reference here.

_____

Language Arts/Literature

(Read or Study for 30 min.)

Topic of Study:_____

Notes, creative writing, summary, poetry

_____

_____

_____

_____

_____

_____

_____

_____

_____

Vocabulary Look Up

_____

_____

_____

_____

History

(Read for 20-30 min.)

Topic of Study:_____

What did you learn today?

_____

_____

_____

_____

_____

_____

Draw a picture from your studies.

Science

(Read 20-30 min)

Topic of Study:_____

What did you learn today?

_____

_____

_____

_____

_____

_____

_____

Draw a picture from your studies.

Math

(Work for 45min-1hr)

Check when done_____

Use this page to work out problems.

Elective
(Work for 30 min)

Topic of Study:_____

Show an adult what you learned today. Write or draw about it here.

Elective
(Work for 30 min)

Topic of Study:_____

Show an adult what you learned today. Write or draw about it here.

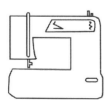

Date : _____   Day 68

Bible Time

(Read for 20 min. in your bible)

Summarize in your own words what you read today.

_____

_____

_____

_____

_____

_____

_____

_____

_____

_____

_____

Scripture reference here.

_____

Language Arts/Literature

(Read or Study for 30 min.)

Topic of Study:_____

Notes, creative writing, summary, poetry

_____

_____

_____

_____

_____

_____

_____

_____

_____

_____

Vocabulary Look Up

_____

_____

_____

_____

_____

History

(Read for 20-30 min.)

Topic of Study:_____

What did you learn today?

_____

_____

_____

_____

_____

Draw a picture from your studies.

Science

(Read 20-30 min)

Topic of Study:_____

What did you learn today?

_____

_____

_____

_____

_____

_____

_____

Draw a picture from your studies.

Math

(Work for 45min-1hr)

Check when done_____

Use this page to work out problems.

Elective

(Work for 30 min)

Topic of Study:_____

Show an adult what you learned today. Write or draw about it here.

Elective

(Work for 30 min)

Topic of Study:_____

Show an adult what you learned today. Write or draw about it here.

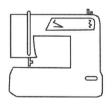

Date :_____   Day 69

Bible Time

(Read for 20 min. in your bible)

Summarize in your own words what you read today.

_____

_____

_____

_____

_____

_____

_____

_____

_____

_____

_____

_____

Scripture reference here.

_____

Language Arts/Literature

(Read or Study for 30 min.)

Topic of Study:_____

Notes, creative writing, summary, poetry

_____

_____

_____

_____

_____

_____

_____

_____

_____

Vocabulary Look Up

_____

_____

_____

_____

History

(Read for 20-30 min.)

Topic of Study:_____

What did you learn today?

_____

_____

_____

_____

_____

Draw a picture from your studies.

Science

(Read 20-30 min)

Topic of Study:_____

What did you learn today?

_____

_____

_____

_____

_____

_____

_____

Draw a picture from your studies.

Math

(Work for 45min-1hr)

Check when done_____

Use this page to work out problems.

Elective

(Work for 30 min)

Topic of Study:_____

Show an adult what you learned today. Write or draw about it here.

Elective

(Work for 30 min)

Topic of Study:_____

Show an adult what you learned today. Write or draw about it here.

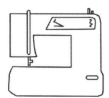

Bible Time

(Read for 20 min. in your bible)

Summarize in your own words what you read today.

_____

_____

_____

_____

_____

_____

_____

_____

_____

_____

_____

_____

Scripture reference here.

_____

Language Arts/Literature

(Read or Study for 30 min.)

Topic of Study:_____

Notes, creative writing, summary, poetry

_____

_____

_____

_____

_____

_____

_____

_____

_____

_____

Vocabulary Look Up

_____

_____

_____

_____

_____

History

(Read for 20-30 min.)

Topic of Study:_____

What did you learn today?

_____

_____

_____

_____

_____

_____

Draw a picture from your studies.

Science
(Read 20-30 min)

Topic of Study: _____

What did you learn today?

_____

_____

_____

_____

_____

_____

_____

Draw a picture from your studies.

Math

(Work for 45min-1hr)

Check when done_____

Use this page to work out problems.

Elective

(Work for 30 min)

Topic of Study:_____

Show an adult what you learned today. Write or draw about it here.

Elective

(Work for 30 min)

Topic of Study:_____

Show an adult what you learned today. Write or draw about it here.

Date :_____   Day 71

Bible Time

(Read for 20 min. in your bible)

Summarize in your own words what you read today.

_____
_____
_____
_____
_____
_____
_____
_____
_____
_____
_____
_____

Scripture reference here.

_____

Language Arts/Literature
(Read or Study for 30 min.)

Topic of Study:_____

Notes, creative writing, summary, poetry

_____

_____

_____

_____

_____

_____

_____

_____

_____

_____

Vocabulary Look Up

_____

_____

_____

_____

History

(Read for 20-30 min.)

Topic of Study:_____

What did you learn today?

_____

_____

_____

_____

_____

_____

Draw a picture from your studies.

Science

(Read 20-30 min)

Topic of Study:_____

What did you learn today?

_____

_____

_____

_____

_____

_____

_____

Draw a picture from your studies.

Math

(Work for 45min-1hr)

Check when done_____

Use this page to work out problems.

Elective
(Work for 30 min)

Topic of Study:_____

Show an adult what you learned today. Write or draw about it here.

Elective
(Work for 30 min)

Topic of Study:_____

Show an adult what you learned today. Write or draw about it here.

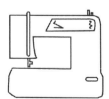

Date :_____   Day 72

Bible Time

(Read for 20 min. in your bible)

Summarize in your own words what you read today.

_____

_____

_____

_____

_____

_____

_____

_____

_____

_____

_____

Scripture reference here.

_____

Language Arts/Literature

(Read or Study for 30 min.)

Topic of Study:_____

Notes, creative writing, summary, poetry

_____

_____

_____

_____

_____

_____

_____

_____

_____

Vocabulary Look Up

_____

_____

_____

_____

History

(Read for 20-30 min.)

Topic of Study:_____

What did you learn today?

_____

_____

_____

_____

_____

Draw a picture from your studies.

Science

(Read 20-30 min)

Topic of Study:_____

What did you learn today?

_____

_____

_____

_____

_____

_____

_____

Draw a picture from your studies.

Math

(Work for 45min-1hr)

Check when done_____

Use this page to work out problems.

Elective

(Work for 30 min)

Topic of Study:_____

Show an adult what you learned today. Write or draw about it here.

Elective

(Work for 30 min)

Topic of Study:_____

Show an adult what you learned today. Write or draw about it here.

Date :_____   Day 73

Bible Time

(Read for 20 min. in your bible)

Summarize in your own words what you read today.

_____
_____
_____
_____
_____
_____
_____
_____
_____
_____
_____
_____

Scripture reference here.

_____

Language Arts/Literature

(Read or Study for 30 min.)

Topic of Study:_____

Notes, creative writing, summary, poetry

_____

_____

_____

_____

_____

_____

_____

_____

_____

_____

Vocabulary Look Up

_____

_____

_____

_____

_____

History

(Read for 20-30 min.)

Topic of Study:_____

What did you learn today?

_____

_____

_____

_____

_____

Draw a picture from your studies.

Science

(Read 20-30 min)

Topic of Study:_____

What did you learn today?

_____

_____

_____

_____

_____

_____

_____

Draw a picture from your studies.

Math

(Work for 45min-1hr)

Check when done_____

Use this page to work out problems.

Elective

(Work for 30 min)

Topic of Study:_____

Show an adult what you learned today. Write or draw about it here.

Elective

(Work for 30 min)

Topic of Study:_____

Show an adult what you learned today. Write or draw about it here.

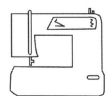

Date :_____   Day 74

Bible Time

(Read for 20 min. in your bible)

Summarize in your own words what you read today.

_____

_____

_____

_____

_____

_____

_____

_____

_____

_____

_____

_____

Scripture reference here.

_____

Language Arts/Literature

(Read or Study for 30 min.)

Topic of Study:_____

Notes, creative writing, summary, poetry

_____

_____

_____

_____

_____

_____

_____

_____

_____

_____

Vocabulary Look Up

_____

_____

_____

_____

History

(Read for 20-30 min.)

Topic of Study:_____

What did you learn today?

_____

_____

_____

_____

_____

Draw a picture from your studies.

Science

(Read 20-30 min)

Topic of Study:_____

What did you learn today?

_____

_____

_____

_____

_____

_____

_____

Draw a picture from your studies.

Math

(Work for 45min-1hr)

Check when done_____

Use this page to work out problems.

Elective

(Work for 30 min)

Topic of Study:_____

Show an adult what you learned today. Write or draw about it here.

Elective

(Work for 30 min)

Topic of Study:_____

Show an adult what you learned today. Write or draw about it here.

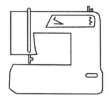

Date :_____   Day 75

Bible Time

(Read for 20 min. in your bible)

Summarize in your own words what you read today.

_____

_____

_____

_____

_____

_____

_____

_____

_____

_____

_____

_____

Scripture reference here.

_____

Language Arts/Literature

(Read or Study for 30 min.)

Topic of Study:_____

Notes, creative writing, summary, poetry

_____
_____
_____
_____
_____
_____
_____
_____
_____
_____

Vocabulary Look Up

_____
_____
_____
_____
_____

History

(Read for 20-30 min.)

Topic of Study:_____

What did you learn today?

_____

_____

_____

_____

_____

_____

Draw a picture from your studies.

Science

(Read 20-30 min)

Topic of Study:_____

What did you learn today?

_____

_____

_____

_____

_____

_____

_____

Draw a picture from your studies.

Math

(Work for 45min-1hr)

Check when done_____

Use this page to work out problems.

Elective

(Work for 30 min)

Topic of Study:_____

Show an adult what you learned today. Write or draw about it here.

Elective

(Work for 30 min)

Topic of Study:_____

Show an adult what you learned today. Write or draw about it here.

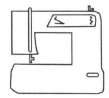

Date : _____   Day 76

Bible Time

(Read for 20 min. in your bible)

Summarize in your own words what you read today.

_____

_____

_____

_____

_____

_____

_____

_____

_____

_____

_____

_____

Scripture reference here.

_____

Language Arts/Literature

(Read or Study for 30 min.)

Topic of Study:_____

Notes, creative writing, summary, poetry

_____

_____

_____

_____

_____

_____

_____

_____

_____

Vocabulary Look Up

_____

_____

_____

_____

History

(Read for 20-30 min.)

Topic of Study:_____

What did you learn today?

_____

_____

_____

_____

_____

_____

Draw a picture from your studies.

Science

(Read 20-30 min)

Topic of Study:_____

What did you learn today?

_____

_____

_____

_____

_____

_____

_____

Draw a picture from your studies.

Math

(Work for 45min-1hr)

Check when done_____

Use this page to work out problems.

Elective
(Work for 30 min)

Topic of Study:＿＿＿＿＿＿＿＿＿＿＿

Show an adult what you learned today. Write or draw about it here.

Elective
(Work for 30 min)

Topic of Study:＿＿＿＿＿＿＿＿＿＿＿

Show an adult what you learned today. Write or draw about it here.

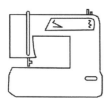

Date : _____   Day 77

Bible Time

(Read for 20 min. in your bible)

Summarize in your own words what you read today.

_____

_____

_____

_____

_____

_____

_____

_____

_____

_____

_____

Scripture reference here.

_____

Language Arts/Literature

(Read or Study for 30 min.)

Topic of Study:_____

Notes, creative writing, summary, poetry

_____

_____

_____

_____

_____

_____

_____

_____

_____

_____

Vocabulary Look Up

_____

_____

_____

_____

_____

History

(Read for 20-30 min.)

Topic of Study:_____

What did you learn today?

_____

_____

_____

_____

_____

Draw a picture from your studies.

Science

(Read 20-30 min)

Topic of Study:_____

What did you learn today?

_____

_____

_____

_____

_____

_____

_____

_____

Draw a picture from your studies.

Math

(Work for 45min-1hr)

Check when done_____

Use this page to work out problems.

Elective

(Work for 30 min)

Topic of Study:_____

Show an adult what you learned today. Write or draw about it here.

Elective

(Work for 30 min)

Topic of Study:_____

Show an adult what you learned today. Write or draw about it here.

Date :_____   Day 78

Bible Time

(Read for 20 min. in your bible)

Summarize in your own words what you read today.

_____

_____

_____

_____

_____

_____

_____

_____

_____

_____

_____

Scripture reference here.

_____

Language Arts/Literature

(Read or Study for 30 min.)

Topic of Study:_____

Notes, creative writing, summary, poetry

_____

_____

_____

_____

_____

_____

_____

_____

_____

_____

Vocabulary Look Up

_____

_____

_____

_____

_____

History

(Read for 20-30 min.)

Topic of Study:_____

What did you learn today?

_____

_____

_____

_____

_____

_____

Draw a picture from your studies.

Science

(Read 20-30 min)

Topic of Study: _____

What did you learn today?

_____

_____

_____

_____

_____

_____

_____

_____

Draw a picture from your studies.

Math

(Work for 45min-1hr)

Check when done_____

Use this page to work out problems.

Elective
(Work for 30 min)

Topic of Study:_____

Show an adult what you learned today. Write or draw about it here.

Elective
(Work for 30 min)

Topic of Study:_____

Show an adult what you learned today. Write or draw about it here.

Date :_____   Day 79

Bible Time

(Read for 20 min. in your bible)

Summarize in your own words what you read today.

_____

_____

_____

_____

_____

_____

_____

_____

_____

_____

_____

_____

Scripture reference here.

_____

Language Arts/Literature

(Read or Study for 30 min.)

Topic of Study:_____

Notes, creative writing, summary, poetry

_____

_____

_____

_____

_____

_____

_____

_____

_____

_____

_____

Vocabulary Look Up

_____

_____

_____

_____

_____

History

(Read for 20-30 min.)

Topic of Study:_____

What did you learn today?

_____

_____

_____

_____

_____

_____

Draw a picture from your studies.

Science

(Read 20-30 min)

Topic of Study:_____

What did you learn today?

_____

_____

_____

_____

_____

_____

_____

Draw a picture from your studies.

Math

(Work for 45min-1hr)

Check when done_____

Use this page to work out problems.

Elective
(Work for 30 min)

Topic of Study:_____

Show an adult what you learned today. Write or draw about it here.

Elective
(Work for 30 min)

Topic of Study:_____

Show an adult what you learned today. Write or draw about it here.

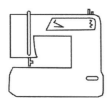

Date : _____   Day 80

Bible Time

(Read for 20 min. in your bible)

Summarize in your own words what you read today.

_____

_____

_____

_____

_____

_____

_____

_____

_____

_____

_____

_____

Scripture reference here.

_____

Language Arts/Literature

(Read or Study for 30 min.)

Topic of Study:_____

Notes, creative writing, summary, poetry

_____

_____

_____

_____

_____

_____

_____

_____

_____

_____

Vocabulary Look Up

_____

_____

_____

_____

History

(Read for 20-30 min.)

Topic of Study:_____

What did you learn today?

_____

_____

_____

_____

_____

Draw a picture from your studies.

Science

(Read 20-30 min)

Topic of Study:_____

What did you learn today?

_____

_____

_____

_____

_____

_____

_____

Draw a picture from your studies.

Math

(Work for 45min-1hr)

Check when done_____

Use this page to work out problems.

Elective
(Work for 30 min)

Topic of Study:_____

Show an adult what you learned today. Write or draw about it here.

Elective
(Work for 30 min)

Topic of Study:_____

Show an adult what you learned today. Write or draw about it here.

Date :_____   Day 82

Bible Time

(Read for 20 min. in your bible)

Summarize in your own words what you read today.

_____

_____

_____

_____

_____

_____

_____

_____

_____

_____

_____

Scripture reference here.

_____

Language Arts/Literature

(Read or Study for 30 min.)

Topic of Study:_____

Notes, creative writing, summary, poetry

_____

_____

_____

_____

_____

_____

_____

_____

_____

Vocabulary Look Up

_____

_____

_____

_____

History

(Read for 20-30 min.)

Topic of Study:_____

What did you learn today?

_____

_____

_____

_____

_____

Draw a picture from your studies.

Science

(Read 20-30 min)

Topic of Study:_____

What did you learn today?

_____

_____

_____

_____

_____

_____

_____

_____

Draw a picture from your studies.

Math

(Work for 45min-1hr)

Check when done_____

Use this page to work out problems.

Elective

(Work for 30 min)

Topic of Study:_____

Show an adult what you learned today. Write or draw about it here.

Elective

(Work for 30 min)

Topic of Study:_____

Show an adult what you learned today. Write or draw about it here.

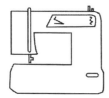

Date : _____   Day 83

Bible Time

(Read for 20 min. in your bible)

Summarize in your own words what you read today.

_____
_____
_____
_____
_____
_____
_____
_____
_____
_____
_____

Scripture reference here.

_____

Language Arts/Literature

(Read or Study for 30 min.)

Topic of Study:_____

Notes, creative writing, summary, poetry

_____

_____

_____

_____

_____

_____

_____

_____

_____

_____

Vocabulary Look Up

_____

_____

_____

_____

_____

History

(Read for 20-30 min.)

Topic of Study:_____

What did you learn today?

_____

_____

_____

_____

_____

Draw a picture from your studies.

Science

(Read 20-30 min)

Topic of Study:_____

What did you learn today?

_____

_____

_____

_____

_____

_____

_____

Draw a picture from your studies.

Math

(Work for 45min-1hr)

Check when done_____

Use this page to work out problems.

Elective

(Work for 30 min)

Topic of Study:_____

Show an adult what you learned today. Write or draw about it here.

Elective

(Work for 30 min)

Topic of Study:_____

Show an adult what you learned today. Write or draw about it here.

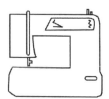

Date :_____   Day 84

Bible Time

(Read for 20 min. in your bible)

Summarize in your own words what you read today.

_____

_____

_____

_____

_____

_____

_____

_____

_____

_____

_____

Scripture reference here.

_____

Language Arts/Literature

(Read or Study for 30 min.)

Topic of Study:_____

Notes, creative writing, summary, poetry

_____

_____

_____

_____

_____

_____

_____

_____

_____

Vocabulary Look Up

_____

_____

_____

_____

_____

History

(Read for 20-30 min.)

Topic of Study:_____

What did you learn today?

_____

_____

_____

_____

_____

Draw a picture from your studies.

Science

(Read 20-30 min)

Topic of Study:_____

What did you learn today?

_____

_____

_____

_____

_____

_____

_____

Draw a picture from your studies.

Math

(Work for 45min-1hr)

Check when done_____

Use this page to work out problems.

Elective
(Work for 30 min)

Topic of Study:_____

Show an adult what you learned today. Write or draw about it here.

Elective
(Work for 30 min)

Topic of Study:_____

Show an adult what you learned today. Write or draw about it here.

Date :_____   Day 85

Bible Time

(Read for 20 min. in your bible)

Summarize in your own words what you read today.

_____

_____

_____

_____

_____

_____

_____

_____

_____

_____

_____

Scripture reference here.

_____

Language Arts/Literature

(Read or Study for 30 min.)

Topic of Study:_____

Notes, creative writing, summary, poetry

_____

_____

_____

_____

_____

_____

_____

_____

_____

_____

Vocabulary Look Up

_____

_____

_____

_____

_____

History

(Read for 20-30 min.)

Topic of Study:_____

What did you learn today?

_____

_____

_____

_____

_____

Draw a picture from your studies.

Science

(Read 20-30 min)

Topic of Study: _____

What did you learn today?

_____

_____

_____

_____

_____

_____

_____

Draw a picture from your studies.

Math

(Work for 45min-1hr)

Check when done_____

Use this page to work out problems.

Elective

(Work for 30 min)

Topic of Study:_____

Show an adult what you learned today. Write or draw about it here.

Elective

(Work for 30 min)

Topic of Study:_____

Show an adult what you learned today. Write or draw about it here.

Date : _____   Day 86

Bible Time

(Read for 20 min. in your bible)

Summarize in your own words what you read today.

_____

_____

_____

_____

_____

_____

_____

_____

_____

_____

_____

Scripture reference here.

_____

Language Arts/Literature

(Read or Study for 30 min.)

Topic of Study:_____

Notes, creative writing, summary, poetry

_____

_____

_____

_____

_____

_____

_____

_____

_____

Vocabulary Look Up

_____

_____

_____

_____

_____

History

(Read for 20-30 min.)

Topic of Study:_____

What did you learn today?

_____

_____

_____

_____

_____

_____

Draw a picture from your studies.

<u>Science</u>

(Read 20-30 min)

Topic of Study:_____

What did you learn today?

_____

_____

_____

_____

_____

_____

_____

Draw a picture from your studies.

Math

(Work for 45min-1hr)

Check when done_____

Use this page to work out problems.

Elective

(Work for 30 min)

Topic of Study:_____

Show an adult what you learned today. Write or draw about it here.

Elective

(Work for 30 min)

Topic of Study:_____

Show an adult what you learned today. Write or draw about it here.

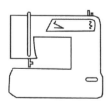

Date :_____   Day 87

Bible Time

(Read for 20 min. in your bible)

Summarize in your own words what you read today.

_____

_____

_____

_____

_____

_____

_____

_____

_____

_____

Scripture reference here.

_____

Language Arts/Literature

(Read or Study for 30 min.)

Topic of Study:_____

Notes, creative writing, summary, poetry

_____

_____

_____

_____

_____

_____

_____

_____

_____

_____

Vocabulary Look Up

_____

_____

_____

_____

_____

History

(Read for 20-30 min.)

Topic of Study: _____

What did you learn today?

_____

_____

_____

_____

_____

Draw a picture from your studies.

Science

(Read 20-30 min)

Topic of Study:_____

What did you learn today?

_____

_____

_____

_____

_____

_____

_____

Draw a picture from your studies.

Math

(Work for 45min-1hr)

Check when done_____

Use this page to work out problems.

Elective

(Work for 30 min)

Topic of Study:_____

Show an adult what you learned today. Write or draw about it here.

Elective

(Work for 30 min)

Topic of Study:_____

Show an adult what you learned today. Write or draw about it here.

Date : _____   Day 88

Bible Time

(Read for 20 min. in your bible)

Summarize in your own words what you read today.

_____

_____

_____

_____

_____

_____

_____

_____

_____

_____

_____

Scripture reference here.

_____

Language Arts/Literature

(Read or Study for 30 min.)

Topic of Study:_____

Notes, creative writing, summary, poetry

_____

_____

_____

_____

_____

_____

_____

_____

_____

Vocabulary Look Up

_____

_____

_____

_____

_____

History

(Read for 20-30 min.)

Topic of Study:_____

What did you learn today?

_____

_____

_____

_____

_____

Draw a picture from your studies.

Science

(Read 20-30 min)

Topic of Study:_____

What did you learn today?

_____

_____

_____

_____

_____

_____

_____

Draw a picture from your studies.

Math

(Work for 45min-1hr)

Check when done_____

Use this page to work out problems.

Elective

(Work for 30 min)

Topic of Study:_____

Show an adult what you learned today. Write or draw about it here.

Elective

(Work for 30 min)

Topic of Study:_____

Show an adult what you learned today. Write or draw about it here.

Date : _____   Day 89

Bible Time

(Read for 20 min. in your bible)

Summarize in your own words what you read today.

_____

_____

_____

_____

_____

_____

_____

_____

_____

_____

_____

Scripture reference here.

_____

Language Arts/Literature

(Read or Study for 30 min.)

Topic of Study:_____

Notes, creative writing, summary, poetry

_____

_____

_____

_____

_____

_____

_____

_____

_____

Vocabulary Look Up

_____

_____

_____

_____

History

(Read for 20-30 min.)

Topic of Study: _____

What did you learn today?

_____

_____

_____

_____

_____

_____

Draw a picture from your studies.

<u>Science</u>
(Read 20-30 min)

Topic of Study:_____

What did you learn today?

_____

_____

_____

_____

_____

_____

_____

Draw a picture from your studies.

Math

(Work for 45min-1hr)

Check when done_____

Use this page to work out problems.

Elective

(Work for 30 min)

Topic of Study:_____

Show an adult what you learned today. Write or draw about it here.

Elective

(Work for 30 min)

Topic of Study:_____

Show an adult what you learned today. Write or draw about it here.

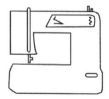

Date :_____   Day 90

Bible Time

(Read for 20 min. in your bible)

Summarize in your own words what you read today.

_____

_____

_____

_____

_____

_____

_____

_____

_____

_____

_____

Scripture reference here.

_____

Language Arts/Literature

(Read or Study for 30 min.)

Topic of Study:_____

Notes, creative writing, summary, poetry

_____

_____

_____

_____

_____

_____

_____

_____

_____

_____

Vocabulary Look Up

_____

_____

_____

_____

History

(Read for 20-30 min.)

Topic of Study:_____

What did you learn today?

_____

_____

_____

_____

_____

Draw a picture from your studies.

Science

(Read 20-30 min)

Topic of Study:_____

What did you learn today?

_____

_____

_____

_____

_____

_____

_____

Draw a picture from your studies.

Math

(Work for 45min-1hr)

Check when done_____

Use this page to work out problems.

Elective
(Work for 30 min)

Topic of Study:_____

Show an adult what you learned today. Write or draw about it here.

Elective
(Work for 30 min)

Topic of Study:_____

Show an adult what you learned today. Write or draw about it here.

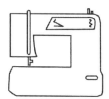

Report

Title:_____

Author:_____Illustrator:_____

_____

_____

_____

_____

_____

_____

_____

_____

_____

_____

_____

_____

_____

_____

_____

_____

_____

_____

_____

_____

_____

_____

_____

_____

_____

_____

_____

_____

_____

_____

_____

_____

By:_____

Report

Title:_____

Author:_____Illustrator:_____

_____

_____

_____

_____

_____

_____

_____

_____

_____

_____

_____

_____

_____

_____

_____

_____

_____

_____

_____

_____

_____

_____

_____

_____

_____

_____

_____

_____

_____

_____

_____

By:_____

Report

Title:_____

Author:_____Illustrator:_____

_____

_____

_____

_____

_____

_____

_____

_____

_____

_____

_____

_____

_____

_____

_____

By:_____

Report

Title:_____

Author:_____Illustrator:_____

_____

_____

_____

_____

_____

_____

_____

_____

_____

_____

_____

_____

_____

_____

By:_____

Congratulations on finishing your 90 days of guided lessons!

A Christian
High School
Delight Directed
Curriculum

If you have completed book 1 and 2 then you have completed 180 schools days!

Date:_____

Parents signature:_____

Copyright

This curriculum is for your family only please do not copy
or sell any parts of this book.
Thank You.

Made in the USA
San Bernardino, CA
17 July 2019